The Price for a Poet is Death
What a Bargain

Also by boB Henning

Traveling at the Speed of Darkness, Poems, © 2009
Nothing to Mend, Music Album, © 2003
Grandfather's Mirror, Music Album, © 1995

Streaming & downloading music available at ReverbNation®
On Spotify® and most other platforms
© boB Henning><Mirror Image Music

The Price for a Poet is Death
What a Bargain

Poems & Selected Lyrics
by
boB Henning

Copyright © 2019 boB Henning
All rights reserved. No part of this publication may be reproduced, stored in or introduced into a retrieval system, or transmitted in any form or by any means, electronic, mechanical, photocopying, recording or otherwise, without the prior written permission of the copyright holder.

16 15 14 13 12 11 10 9 8 7 6 5 4 3 2

Second Printing, 2020

ISBN 978-0-578-45761-1

Publication and Copy Editor: Tracy Catanese

Cover design: Tracy Catanese

Back cover author photograph: *grandboB & JS3*, © 2015 Michelle Henning So

Front cover watercolor: *Juicy Water Weeds*, © 2009 Jennifer Martin, courtesy of the artist
Check out Jennifer's work on LinkedIn. Jennifer has the heart of a visual artist, with a calling and career as a Sustainable Energy Educator.

For Craig Porter (1974–2011)

His gentle voice is in the whirling wind now.
The autumn breeze — his renewable realm.
The flutter of leaves — his most eloquent song.

Preface

With an incontinent imagination and a muse forever tossing grains of sand at your window – well, sometimes it's a challenge to hold it, and to hold it all together. Creative individuals, whether they are visual artists, musicians, comedians, actors or writers, do count in their numbers quite a few who live near the edge. Each of us can name the names of those who have jumped or fallen into the abyss, not to return. Many more of us swirl about this gyre, in lesser or greater degrees of turmoil, and are spared, frequently through no feat of our own.

Coming back from the precipice can offer a new perspective on life, love and death for some. Those of you, who have been there, many more than once, know exactly to what I am referring. The dream-world elements of mythos, enchantment and mystery take on a greater significance in waking life. And if we are fortunate, we may even bring back something inimitably precious: a tune; a lyric; an image; a tale; a joke; a poem. It may be right away or much later. Our sense of timing is irrelevant to the god Mercury.

Somehow love is entangled in all of this mortality stuff. Emily Dickinson wrote, "If I can stop one heart from breaking, I shall not live in vain." People do die of broken hearts. The modern usage of *La petite mort* is evidential. Dickinson further wrote, "Love – is anterior to Life – Posterior – to Death…" And, the power of duende is forgotten at great peril. Finally, there are those who even go so far as to say that it is difficult to love another genuinely without at least a little consideration being given to one's own mortality.

More than a few of my new poems in this collection are interrelated with this unreasonable, crazy pair, love and death. The rest of the poems and prose poems (and lyrics from my previous albums) are simply one or the other or just not.

Of the Gaelic inscription inspiring the title itself, there is a multiplicity of interpretation: that the price for being a poet is some nature of death; the price for loving a poet the same. Just ask those who are poets. And certainly ask those who risk the love of a poet.

The cost to be a poet or "obtain" a poet is frequently the equivalent. Throw in the Trickster, and absolutely interject humor (amusing), and something intriguing might keep us stirring for at least a little while longer!

— the author

CONTENTS

Dedication

Preface

Gaelic Inscription and Graffiti

Poems

1	After November	2
2	Luna Moth	3
3	#11 What's the Solution?	3
4	Warm Cookies	4
5	Russian Roulette	5
6	My Mother at Eighty-Six	6
7	Questions for Dad	7
8	Molten	9
9	Countdown	11
10	Proud Americans	11
11	Snapdragon	12
12	Meniere's Syndrome	13
13	I and the Land are One	17
14	The Event Horizon	18
15	En Route to My Mother's Burial on June 24, 2010…	18
16	It's Easy to Misinterpret a Poet…	19
17	Moving My Small Hut Closer to Sunset	20
18	*Oh! Do You Know the Muffin Man?*	21
19	A Tree Ring	22
20	Sand	23
21	Discontent	24
22	Cat Scratch	24
23	To My Enemy	25
24	Love and Death	25
25	Adorable Gypsy	26
26	*Don't Fade on Me*	26

27	Robert Bly Requests a Poem of What I Want	27
28	Fond Memories – As the Dog that is You Licks…	28
29	Veiled Encounter	29
30	Alike	29
31	Dream Girl	30
32	Feathers	31
33	Lady of the Lake	32
34	All Weather Friend	33
35	*What Was Said to the Rose*	33
36	Birthday Gifts	34
37	The Time of Change	35
38	Last Night's Dream	36
39	Waking Up	36
40	Two Days Before My Son Kyle's Graduation	37
41	#6 What's the Solution?	38
42	Great Mother	38
43	Crossed Fingers	39
44	Grounding	40
45	Maple Seed	41
46	Milkweed	41
47	Fresh Air	42
48	Four Hours of Lightning	42
49	This Mountain	43
50	This Loneliness	44
51	Not Writing Poetry	45
52	Line Dancing	46
53	Lichens	46
54	Table Clock	47
55	Honoring Those in Uniform	48

Prose Poems

The Forest Where I Lived	52
Headline: POETS FORCED TO EAT THEIR OWN WORDS	53
The Hatfield	55

Selected Lyrics from Music Projects

Grandfather's Mirror©
    Grandfather's Mirror   58
    Legendary Bridge   59
    A Place to Call Your Own   60
    Soulmates   60

Nothing to Mend©
    Shadow   61
    You (A Solace)   62
    I'm Not Down With Clowns   63
    Bugs on Drugs   64

Online
    You're My Irish Blessing   65
    Help Not Wanted (Pronoia)   66

Gratitude

There is a spell of death in mocking a poet.

It is surefire death to love a poet.

And the most certain death is to be a poet.

– Gaelic inscription (late 8th century)

Aphrodite + Thanatos

– Graffiti spray-painted
under the Meridian St. bridge
over the White River
in Indianapolis

POEMS

After November
in memory of Craig Porter

Back in the still air of a summer solar noon
a slightly hunched green shoot of a man once stood
wearing a pall over dirty yellow silks:
he's now baffled to the ground this forlorn season.

The wind has howled for days
up the Wabash River Valley
and increasingly along the lonely thin furrow
where smiles once articulated a woman's face.

Grains of topsoil skip uncontrolled
along the crushed brown husks
of trampled corn stalks that now whisper grief
in their parched post-November way.

The gusting halts to flutters before recurring
without regard for this fallow field
where answers lie in barrenness
hiding shadow-bearing seeds.

A petite tassel curls lovingly
around a tear-wetted field-stone:
her precocious love searching the broken soil
for this small comfort of his unbroken forte.

From a high place feathers furl
and quiver slightly at their winglets:
a salutation to the man and his dream
sustained by she who struggles on.

Luna Moth

Once after egg a carpet-bagging, upholstered worm
then concealed in a chrysalis of your own creation
'til emerging with proboscis and feathered antennae.
Have you received now my telepathic invitation?

Your flight here erratic yet resolute
clinging with dark legs
on the bark of a Maine forest White Pine
shimmery in the full moonlight of May.

Distracting dark eyes
spot each swept wing
and your hidden small set
with which you really see.

Your pastel green wings
weightless and powdery
last night of your life
you expend with me.

#11 What's the Solution?

Bigger diggers can be found.
But none is finer than this miner.

Warm Cookies

I want to be loved
like you love cookies.
I want to love you
like I love cookies too.

The way you suddenly sense
cookies baking nearby.
The way you breathe in their sweetness
like nothing else in life mattered.

How you check an entire pan
and see that certain one.
How you reach out and clutch
your discrete choice with care.

The delight of just-baked cookies
an aroma drawing us close.
Does it not make sense to want cookies
everywhere in our lives?

There is no aggression in a cookie.
Any day's bitter taste is calmed.
Perhaps that deep comfort of cookies
is that something which feels like home.

I would like a cookie
before I walk up the next hill.
And I would really like one more cookie
before…I go…downhill.

Russian Roulette

I order a Saturday night *Amazon* special:
a copy of Dickman's book of poetry,
Mayakovsky's Revolver,
from a woman at Princeton.

I never receive the book.
I peruse it revolving
from Pennsylvania to New Jersey
and then a dead end in Cincinnati.

Did the Postal Inspector
find it dangerous to handle;
Homeland Security x-rays imagine
an unlicensed handgun on the cover;

was the ISBN filed off the back?
I guess it's plausible considering
the city's record murder rate and now
it's likely confined with dead letters.

I subsequently secure another
and having traveled a different track
it actually shot right through
rain, snow and blood to me.

After reading it I was going to
loan it out in Indianapolis
without the permission of the authorities.
Doubtless I know it wouldn't be returned.

Instead, spine reversed it's on my bookshelf
between poets Tsvetaeva, Akhmadulina,
Akhmatova and Pasternak
concealed just in case I need defense.

My Mother at Eighty-Six

She fell many times
showing us how to skate
above the cold lost faces of dropped coins
and the spiny backs of small-mouth bass
frozen in Silver Lake's downy ice.

And she slid down with us
off our saucers and sleds
over unseen age-old, silt-laden bones
downslope the tree-skirted hill
of Stow's Adel Durbin Park.

But this time she fell
and does not recognize herself
let alone know my father, her husband
who she thinks is the mayor of someplace,
perceiving he must be someone of importance.

Neither does she discern even one
of her so far un-fallen offspring,
nor grasp that our sister, her first-born
has descended a wintry season ago
all the way back down into earth.

The snow drops steadily
outside fractal-frosted windows.
It hangs painfully heavy on the east side of the Blue Spruce
so like the weight of being
on my mother's splintered left hip.

The corners of my father's mouth slant down,
his eyes glazed and hemmed in with crow's feet
as he looks out fidgeting into a midwinter sky
seeming to reminisce some clear air glide
piloting his 'Liberator' in December of '43.

I imagine the water still
surging out from under the edge-ice
over the dam in Munroe Falls
where we resided for so many years
and commenced this journey of falling.

Questions for Dad

My daughter asks her grandfather,
"How did you meet her?"
Her light cheerful voice he cannot hear
from hundreds of hours piloting PT-17s, AT-6s and B-29s.

His conversation goes somewhere
while she says to me, "He didn't hear me."
I wonder, "How many times
I have not heard her myself?"

I suggest that she ask him again
and she defers back to me, so I say,
"Dad. Michelle is interested in
how you met mom."

"Oh...! Well . . . "
And he tells his story,
a chapter I've never heard before
but then again he's an epic 90 years.

"Her brother was a hired hand
on our family farm.
She brought lunch out one day
and that's how it all began."

He finishes his memory
in the course of an hour
and just before he downs
one more gin & tonic

jumps up from his recliner saying,
"Time for dinner, let's go!"
To my sister's farm
just down the road.

We have bottles of wine
and traditional fixings.
Dad sits to my left,
Michelle to my right.

I ask him, "Had enough?"
"Oh, Yes," he lowly murmurs.
as we finish off our meals
and clear a few plates.

The desserts are uncovered.
"Want a slice of pumpkin pie
dad? Dad? Dad? Dad?
…DAD!

Are you all right?"
No response. Chin in chest.
Drooling. Ashen lips.
Round his eyes a grey cast.

My sister pre-grieves his passing. The other calls help.
My daughter phones for counsel from her mother.
The extended family stands in a line near the wall.
I hold his head in my arms and cup his face.

No pulse and no breathing.
Made clear he's No Code.
E.M.T.s arrive
as he suddenly comes to.

"Oh, yes." is his answer
to the call, "You O.K.?"
Thanksgiving is his answer to
 "What is the day?"

A trip to the hospital
and he's back home next day.
"When's your next visit?"
he inquires as I leave.

Soon dad.
Very, very soon.

Molten

The fire dancer
is a-twirl
with flames
her curling
raven blessed
hair entangles
the fire
the night
the lake
the rain
and all transfixed
 creatures about.

Molten streams
of vivacity
flare out of
her dark eyes
soul windows
burst with luminosity
the life
the death
the pain
exorcised with
brilliant creative flames.

Like the sequentially
stalking legs of
a primordial
spider her
blackened garments
adhere
under
her command
uninhibited
Eros
the nature
that is her.

The ash of
hair
and flesh
soak up poison
like charcoal
from some primitive being's
cooking fire
filter the dark water
the lake
night rain
pooling in cisterns
deep within her.

Her sinews
forged to iron
rust to small
furry animals that
scurry off
in all directions.
Branded all over marks
that she belongs in
the conflagration
above the cauldron
of the ancient crafter
of fine metals.

Countdown

Five times
I have died in the arms of Aphrodite.
Forging
like Hephaestus a soul of gold.
Trying, and trying, and trying,
to duel
by myself
once upon my time.

Proud Americans

Snowflakes flutter fall
in *XY* chromosomal forms.
White only genes, colorfast
unaffected by dyeing.

As iron filings
flock to a magnet
to treads these flakes stick
beneath heavy camo boots.

Clodhoppers which traipse
in the blood of schoolchildren
tainted with charcoal
sulfur and saltpeter.

This concoction of blood-snow
is then shaped into crosses
by accomplices called bystanders
who say their tardy prayers.

Snapdragon

The allure
of a closed Snapdragon
pinched open between
the thumb and index finger: Walla!

At age five I did just this once again
with one of my mother's Snapdragons
in the summer sun next to the garage.
And boy was I surprised.

Unlike any Snapdragon before
this particular flower was occupied
and with a startle akin to
opening an unavailable port-o-pot

a Bumble Bee flew directly out at me
whereby I circled the house
tore open the back screen door
and hid safely in the basement.

A week earlier while playing in the field
from a quarter-sized hole in the ground
poured forth a stream of Yellow Jackets
and my mouth and nostril were still hurting.

But in Autumn when the Snapdragons
joined so many other flowers after frost
there remained a unique quality
as the seed pods, skull-shaped, mocked me.

Meniere's Syndrome
...if despair, then not without some quiet hope. Life, however long, will always be short. — Wistawa Szymborska

Abrupt
it arrives after
time on the lam
episodic
fluctuating
rotational vertigo
nausea
capricious commotion
violent convulsions.

The sweaty flashes
hot and cold
spinning as if
flu-ravaged and forced to
ride a Tilt-A-Whirl for
the length of
a school day
seventeen days out of
a month of days.

Ten hours of
dry heaves of
tremors
pressed down
on the cold
stone floor
whirling yet
immobile no
hope.

I wish I was dead.

The eyes say that way
the brain another
and the ears do not agree
vomit rises in
the lava tube hideous
moans horrible
crying out
utter debility
absolutely incapable.

Complete exhaustion
no dignity
stolen away
no care to go
anywhere do
anything fulfill
expectations live
anymore.
Down a drain.

Driving the car suddenly
the whole world shifts
a quarter of a turn to
the right with
wild full spin then
half turn to
the left then
the vilest torture in
erratic motion.

The numbers
of Fibonacci's Ratio
my Cochlea
scrambled
now I'm no use
the ultimate dis
ability no
solution to this
ringing in my ear.

I would rather be dead.

No one grasps
the utter hell
of my disorder
and merely spin tales of
my poor disposition
my incompetence
my faulty self-esteem
my ineptness why I am
the way I am.

Termed
an idiopathic
disease
incurable

barely treatable
unknown
pin-wheeling
out of control
a whorl.

"What can I do for you?
Move you to hospital?"
"NO!"
I am moving already
Don't move me
Don't touch me
Don't make me
explain myself
again.

Cold wet cloth
lightly ever
so lightly on
the forehead
a second on
the back of the
neck
lightly
ever so lightly.

A dabble of water
on the lips
lights low no
noise speak softly
ever so softly.
And then
as if nothing
had happened it
all passes away…for the time… I would like…to live.

I and the Land are One
for Michael Stocker

The atmosphere is confused.

Geese in formation are flying east
as their magnetic brains
keep telling them that they are "going south" –
and they will all die on the Eastern Front.

A whale beaches itself
its ears deaf from naval sonar
its back gouged by propellers
its stomach full of plastic.

A firefly is obliterated
on a headlight
and leaves a dying tracer
on the windshield.

Through smoke I see death
in the eyes of the magician at the pub.
He knows that I see him.
He calls himself "Trinity."

People are confused
and so the spider cannot make mandalas
any
more.

We have forgotten again
to ask The Grail Question
whilst the Fisher King is gravely wounded.

The currents deep in the seas are confused.

The Event Horizon

A detached reconnoitering of the world
has infiltrated humanity.
We revel in our awkwardness
furled up on beaches in globules of oil.

At the top of the company ladder
there is an empty roof
covered with a hot tar membrane
and plenty of edges from which to jump.

Scared and rich, smug authorities
equivalents of mechanized raccoons with croup
bring out our worst, spoiling creation.
Like every Russian novel we need a spring thaw.

The derision of well-paid ranting bullies
impede the movement of the gyre:
the moving walkway is coming to an end,
but let's make-believe that there's no entropy.

En Route to My Mother's Burial on June 24, 2010, I Saw the Dead Poet William Stafford at a *McDonald's*

I saw the poet William Stafford
who died nearly seventeen years ago
sitting in the *McDonald's* this morning
in St. Marys, Ohio.

I was driving to my mother's burial.
His right hand was shaky
and he waited patiently
for a second cup of coffee.

I'm not in the habit
of seeing poets who have died.
Yet there we were
each trying to wake up.

It's Easy to Misinterpret a Poet from the Next Room

*One trouble about language is that people sometimes believe
what you say, and you were only trying it out.* — William Stafford

Strutting as naughty faeries
enchanted insects
consume only religious books on the shelves.
Un-nibbled are all the poems, myth and music.

Hundreds of grasshoppers were reported,
their backs pinioned like hors d'oeuvres.
I suppose that they were escapees
from my neighbor's bug habit.

A child told me that her cat parts the curtain
to a world you will never see
and that all children agree
there are tigers beneath those lilies.

Somebody murdered Pinocchio
in the back seat of my car.
Carved on his snapped splintered nose
was something regarding lying about a big fish.

And to top it all
Jiminy Cricket is impaled on my front grill.
Now every time I blow my horn it chirps
and spontaneously I rub my legs together.

Now for some strange reason
every time I visit friends
they always give me an air mattress
so I can't hide a chainsaw beneath.

Moving My Small Hut Closer to Sunset

A man is lost
far from cool waters
for he has not learned that at times
a nymph yearns for an embrace
not so tight as to sense distress
just enough to feel cozy and safe.

This man's tongue's a parched mudflat
his heart pants more than beats
eyes desiccated and uncertain
he thirsts for a coast and a creature
that will crack the oath he clutches
unshackle the burden he carries.

Yes, I am this man on a quenching quest
more west than east
more dusk than dawn.
Each evening I move
my small hut closer to sunset.
It's quiet there like the moment dew forms.

A girl there named Hesperia lands.
Dressed in charcoal she sifts all clamors.
Peering back at the rising moon
her boat glides away from the shore.
Below the waterline this cloaked maiden
having soaked all sorrow steals away each day.

Oh! Do You Know the Muffin Man?

Fresh from the bakery
dark chocolate muffins
have long aroused my senses
at the Cornerstone Coffeehouse.

These delectable muffins used to be
"Buy One, Get a 2nd half-price."
But now they are
"Buy Two & Get a 3rd 50% off."

Fuck the Muffin Man!

In the food desert
of The Far East Side
"somebody" pushed all the shopping carts
into the nearby retention pond.

Oh, do you happen to *know*
The Muffin Man?
I've heard that he
lives on Drury Lane.

Fuck that Muffin Man!

I received a cake of cocoa
especially baked for me
because it was my birthday
and all my friends were there.

But when I pried open the box
my name was badly misspelled
and you know who I think is behind it?
I want his address on said lane.

Fuck the Muffin Man!

A Tree Ring

In a dark wood I saw – I saw my several selves
Come running from the leaves.   — Theodore Roethke

After nightfall
a ring of renegades
of which I am one
plant Burr Oaks
on abandoned properties

where foreclosed dwellings
remodeled or dilapidated
stand darkened
and lack of trees
make it darker.

Our permission slip
to intrude
approved by
green fire
of an altered Aries heart.

Wearing dusky dungarees,
shirts and gloves,
with our shovels
and mattocks
we dig the murky soil

set a tree
fill the hole
pound in stakes
bamboo or steel
with sledge hammers

protect the trees
from bankers' brush-hogs
sent to mow down everything.
They keep their distance:
no broken blades.

Neighbors call authorities
at the clamor of our work.
Cops don't arrest us
(think we're cray-cray)
say don't trespass – wink, wink.

In the morning
I breathe in
the reminiscent aromas
of sassafras roots
from a cheerful childhood Spring.

My absent parents
ceded me
a family of woodlands.
Now on neglected parcels
saplings dream of water and light.

Sand
      for Michelle & James

Flows through the narrowing
neck of the hourglass marking time.

Specks numerous as
stars blanketing and softening
the edge of our terrestrial
world from that of the sea.

Blown by the wind, carving
the very stone from which it is born covering
ancient treasures and covering our tracks.

Shards of shells and bits
of rocks at the heart
of the wounded pearl.

Castles. Concrete. Chips. Clocks.

Discontent

The day before her servants leave town
she notices the change in their patterns.
She paws at the suitcase and re-marks
her belongings which of course are everything.

Abruptly she runs
an accustomed jagged route
but the couch has just been moved
and out the open window she goes.

Acting as if nothing has transpired
she grooms fastidiously
settling now on the warm car hood –
nice place for a nap all the day long.

Cat Scratch

Again tonight I cannot sleep
as the cat bites at my writing hand.
She knows I now must write.
Persisting she wounds my wrist.

And so like many other nights
I traipse again to my writing desk.

While I scribble she chews the eraser
and paws the paper and delays my labor.

Don't make it any easier,
I pronounce to her
as she pounces on the line
I have just writ . . .

To My Enemy
      For several minutes two mosquitoes have been
      making love on top of this poem. – Galway Kinnell

You are so lovely
as you suck the life out of me.

Your sleek, primordial skill of stealth
attracted to attack me
by my own breath
exhaled into the dusk air.

The instant before my eyes adjust
to the falling darkness
you stab me with precision
and it is over before I know it.

Only after you have filled yourself with me
am I aroused to slap myself
but you have already left me
in sheer madness.

Love and Death

Perhaps it would be preferable
to be that Praying Mantis
who is so enthralled by his femme fatale
that after making love with her

is consumed completely
muttering to oneself that
having just that intensity of affection
would be OK with just such an outcome.

Adorable Gypsy
          after Lorca for Tracy Catanese

Snarky mirth embodied
spiraling raven feathered hair
swirling the mythic stars sizzle
Soror Mystica alchemy.

Steam infused sweat
shooting out fine streams
from tangled strands
circumambulating sassily.

Don't Fade on Me
          in memory of Tom Petty

We're fading away.
We all fade away.
The song fades out.
Don't....fade on me.

The engraving on
my great-great-grandfather's
lichened marble gravestone is
now worn illegible by generations.

The date, mint and words
of a Buffalo Nickel
are worn off completely
by pockets, machines and hands.

The cloth
of the checkered flag
outside this Indianapolis 500 home
has been bleached by sunlight.

Wildflowers and memory fade
but the voice and *Rickenbacker*'s strings
forever resonate across the galaxy.
The magic of Your music never fades.

Robert Bly Requests a Poem of What I Want

I want the obsidian pupils of children
to blaze with a mirthfulness
that reflects grown-ups who actually see them.

I want the envy-fired kiln behind my heart
to be cooled by a wind that has blown
by some distant bog of humility.

I want to pick through my bone-pile of losses
with charred twigs drawn from the edge
of a fire pit concealing my father's ashes.

* * * * * * *

I desire to carouse with that woman
whose powder-yellow scarf of remorse
is loosely tied around the tops of her hip bones.

Iliac crests so soft, yet solid as clarity
those mossy knobs of sprouting caribou antlers
or the long-unappreciated pollen pouches of honey bees.

The woman whose fierce, momentarily retracted claws
fiddle rat bones, willow bark and dried Bluet flowers
in a diminutive doeskin poet's purse
secreted down from Lalla to Anna Akhmatova and now to her.

Fond Memories –
As the Dog that is You Licks My Face

I drove a car backwards
when I was four years old.
We crossed a four-lane highway
did a U-turn and crashed a snow fence.

In the back seat rode a girl and a dog.
Both were three and no one was hurt.
I don't remember the incident.
A spanking blackout and my stinging rear end?

My earliest memory ever
is a solarium, sun fuzzy in my eyes
the swaying shadows of a cluster
of still sleeping trees in Springtime.

A few years pass and I'm hiding beneath
the massive long-deceased tree
leaning in the shade of its descendants
in the forest between Pinehurst and Lyndsey.

Mmm…the luscious aroma arising
out of rough-sawn Black Walnut planks
which once lay curing in the barn loft
from my grandfather's 1920's sawmill.

Slipping sadly into a bisque grown-up
a woman of wander wonders
transformed those wallows by picking
me for her team of two.

Oh the times you excitedly greeted me
while sitting on front porch steps,
restrained in back yards, lying on shop floors
paws all over me: the dog that is you, licked my face.

Veiled Encounter
        in memory of Pierre Boivin

Walking towards her
in the dorm hallway
he surprises a naked coed
just out of the shower room.

She brings a washcloth
to her face with both hands
instinctively
so as to veil her identity.

He sees everything of course
and even a little bit more
for there appear curls of coyness
at the corners of her still visible lips.

Alike

And so they begin that slow dance
of minimal distance.
Lilts of wind lift the strands of hair
nearest her ear.

Light of predawn sky
refracts from the corner of his right eye.
A slight curling of her lip
appears just to the left

at which his breath
intermingles with the vapor of her sigh.
There is a bright glow enveloping this pair
the instant of sunrise.

Dream Girl

You are the third most beautiful woman whom I have ever
        encountered.
If you choose to be offended I understand – it is OK.
But please know this: the other two appeared in my dreams –
and what is a guy supposed to do?

As we connect with our eyes I can plainly see
that I really just want to take you home.
Not my home. And not yours.
Somebody else's home.

We just choose a place that we both like and declare it ours.
It would be fine if it is just a flat.
Or a treehouse.
Or a tent-house we make in someone's living room.

And we order room service – whatever we like
from the residents or the next-door neighbors,
take in their cats, and guinea pigs and children
but not their hissing cockroaches.

I play their guitar.
You proceed to teach me to strum in a better way.
I go to the fridge, take out a brick of Swiss cheese
and try to predetermine where the tunnels will lead.

You eat the cheese right out of my hand
whilst saying that women and men
are like spaces on a checkerboard
and I forget about my little contrived project as you King me.

Feathers
       for Clara DeGalan

Huginn and Muninn fly every day over all the world; I worry for Huginn that he might not return, but I worry for Muninn more.
    — Odin of his Chief Advisor Ravens in the Eddic poem *Grímnismál*

On a clear dusk
a quorum of corvids squawk:
"Caw! Caw! Caw!" <<*Squall's comin'.*>>

The cacophony of crows calms
as the skies of darkened blue crystal
break open with the crackle of thunderclaps.

A spell goes by
and a thunderbolt crashes in an al fresco chapel
guarded by quivering blackbirds.

Uphill on an outcrop of rock
crowned by a birdhouse of dance
beaks peck some candid kisses.

An Uncivilized Spotted Nutcracker
and a Common Raven
have a chance encounter of desire.

Elegantly disguised
and focused on her craft
calm as amber, tranquil as peace.

Ruffled around the edges
and cocking his skull
he listens and scratches out insights.

Will memories come back
and more so desire?
Claws clutch each shoulder for now.

Lady of The Lake

> *There is a lake so tiny that a mustard seed would cover it easily,
> yet everyone drinks from this lake.* — Lalla of Kashmir

Lady of the Lake.
Lady of the Lake
Excalibur's Guardian.
You, like your waters are unbound.

Let us make no
pledges of sensible hearts.
Warm me Lady of the Lake.

Lady of the Lake.
Lady of the Lake
I will not endeavor in vain
to contain you still.

Let us exchange
excessively valued gifts.
Cool me Lady of the Lake.

Lady of the Lake.
Lady of the Lake
so may you lightly shimmer-pour
between my fingers unclenched.

Let us gaze at
our reflection this moment.
Laugh heartily Lady of the Lake.

All Weather Friend
        for Jennifer Martin

I know it sounds like a putdown
but she knows this is not the case.
I tell her again as a compliment
that she is my foul weather friend.

My left-handed compliment
not so sinister
an admiring glance is all I take
and she is my unfair weather friend.

Cobalt skies. Eyes sad.
Shared smiles or slogging miles and miles
with a hope that life will be a little fair.
She is my all weather friend.

What Was Said to the Rose
        for Doug Von Koss

Beaded with dewdrops
your fragrance enfolds me.
Dried between pages
I present heaven's scent.

Birthday Gifts

To the poet who is Captain of our small boat:
a mouse companion whose whiskers are as sleek as Arthur's sword
and whose footpads are as pink as my mother's Coral Bells.

To my generous mother:
two gardens: one in the sun to raise her spirit on a thermal
and the other in the shade to alleviate her weary soul in the ground.

To my father the pilot:
a cloud bank in the valley
that lingers near the wet Walnut trees of dawn.

To my wife the healer:
the energy about the bodies of indigo-flecked angels
dressed in the downy seeds of milkweed.

To my precious daughter:
the purrs of Cleopatra's cats humming near her heart
and the rustling of vivid Autumn leaves scurrying across her mind.

To my eldest son:
a pillow of laughter that percolates when dreamed upon
and conceals a golden blade of bliss.

To my youngest son:
the silver water that fires the stars of Draco
and slants the left chain of Cassiopeia.

To my greatest childhood friend:
a lifetime longer than it was
and shorter than amber from the Caspian Sea.

To my fallen mentor of wind and sun: a leafy jacket
for a bright day, a cricket-chewed knit hat for the breeze
and rain barrels full from the first storm of Spring.

To my sincere renewable partner the doe-eyed painter: a bubble
of glacial air the size of forever embracing
whisker-thin water weeds of a summer lake in the far north.

To my harmonizers in the feminine: a fiddle
for a dancing heart, a bow sliding slow on the nape of the neck
and resonating strings dissipating meaningless woe.

To myself:
steam from a Celtic copper kettle
and four blue flames from a blaze of meteoric ice.

To Mother Earth:
an April with no residual
trace of me but the trees.

The Time of Change

One chief is replaced by another
as Lincoln on his throne
takes over obverse and reverse
of American common cents in 1909.

The sacred buffalo
and another chief on the nickel
are substituted in 1938
by Thomas Jefferson and his stone house.

Mercury dimes
Liberty quarters
Walking half dollars
all are supplanted.

Peace dollars were gone by '35.
A five-star general takes over in '71
a moon his behind
a soaring eagle out in space.

Our change reflects our change.
Once comprised of gold and silver.
Our change reflects our times
now worthless clad steels.

Last Night's Dream

If age were magic
would it be the age that you are now?

Waking Up

Never underestimate the cleverness
of somebody who is no one.
Pollywogs may talk behind your back
and boast about how wonderful you are.

Have you spent too much of your life
fencing in the spinach
so that it didn't chase
the rabbits and groundhogs?

Perhaps at one time
you were that old saloon
where the fan turns slowly
but the *Incredible Hulk* just crapped in the loo.

You may have come from
a long line of multiple personalities.
Seek out a Barred Owl
and question who you are really.

It's time for you to wake up!
The sun has been setting on your life
ever since the very day
that you were born.

Two Days Before My Son Kyle's Graduation

The surface glimmers
in the salt marsh of Charleston
our third and last child
no longer an undergraduate.

Southern Live Oaks sway
with their slow dance partners
of Carolina Spanish Moss
near a reflective brackish surface.

The smooth gleam
that covers my son's eyes
commingles
with the inland waterway.

The paper that says,
'You've Striven.' Go on now!
Let's dance! Dance life's dance.
Unhurriedly – at your own pace.

#6 What's the Solution?

Dancers four in a circle they spin.
One after another yet none will win.

Great Mother

Alone
at nine and more
I myself
inside
a daylight-dappled bramble cave
picked glisten-beaded blackberries
returning home with more than half for
mother.

Alone
at forty-two
my mother
inside
her murky-stifled kitchen cove
baked pies from what her eldest son
surrenders she remembers years of no
mother.

Alone
at quite well-done
my granddad
inside
his shady roadside produce coop
stirred music plucking his guitar
preparing licks with piebald lips for
mother.

Crossed Fingers

You are such a liar. Yes, you!
(And, well, me too.)

All of us are liars.
Fibbers.
Untrue storytellers.
In some way, we are all liars.

Grey lies are close to white lies.
Like how BIG something is.
Hmm...
What I meant was the size of the fish.

Maybe black lies are those of which we are unconscious.
The ones that we have told so often we now believe are so.
And the green ones concern sources of income
including our declarations to the IRS.

Blue lies are about how we answer the pleasantry,
"How are you?"
And the red ones are certainly about love... and not love,
whilst twisting a ring when someone attractive comes into the pub.

The purple lie is a mixture of blue and red ones.
And how old or young you really are.
Would yellow lies be those that we tell our doctors
concerning how often we imbibe and those other things?

Some liars are pathological.
They are probably beige.
Certainly they are not preferable for a position of power
or naïvely relied upon in a relationship.

Shall we keep our fingers crossed
behind our backs
about the white lies
for just a little longer?

Grounding
      for the electrician Rene Schaub

You wake up one day and notice everything is tangled.
Extension cords are at fault.
There they are: knotty cables.
Passionate confused cousins of garden hoses and twisted hair.

Overnight you *know* what they have been doing.

Come on now. How else can there be a snarl like that?
Female and male ends there and there.
They have been making connections.
Plugging and unplugging. Hooking up.

Coiled cables are with trouble lights.
Power strips with currently bare wires.
Desk lamps with loose sockets.
Adapters emotionally involved with exhausted chargers.

Lying about the front lawn like empty six-packs
spent batteries touch face-down plug prongs.
They are conceivably part of some
AC/DC experimentation that didn't go well.

All those heart breakers last night
over-loaded at The Grounding Bar.

It's the morning after.
Evident charges hang-over sparks and sizzles.

Maple Seed

The wisdom of a maple seed
releasing its clutch
alighting to clink
to a great relief below.

The plink inciting memory:
children astride bicycles
spokes clothes-pinned
baseball cards clattering.

Milkweed

Monarchs flutter.
Bees bumble.
Hummingbirds hover.
Ants scent-trek the Milky Way.

Once pungent blossom
now verdant womb
snug fleecy parasols
let go and lilt.

Fresh Air

There's a riotous joviality
in the tree canopy.
Leaves mingle
winds jostle the limbs.

On calm days
each leafy branch
alone
so close make no contact.

But today
there's a stimulating brush
refreshing stir
after such a protracted stifle.

Four Hours of Lightning

When lightning strikes
I forget everything.

When thunder catches up
so do my thoughts.

When the rain comes
I forget my troubles.

When the clouds pass
I recall my real name.

This Mountain
      for Jay Leeming

This mountain is a glacial stone
shoved here over the lifetimes of a turtle's ancestors.

This mountain is father's scarf worn threadbare
much lighter now with snowcaps.

This mountain is a broken Black Oak limb
waiting to notice its lichens as family.

This mountain is a photo of a daughter
etched in phases by the moon.

This mountain is a thread of silver
polished by the tears of a dragonfly.

This mountain is a shimmering Cross Spider's web
shading a fatigued forest ranger in its shadow.

This mountain is a dusky ant
that glimmers in the sun with each switchback.

This mountain is a splinter of Crazy Horse's left leg
waiting to stand again.

This mountain is a meteorite from the ort cloud of dreams
embedded here to ignite a creative heart.

This Loneliness

This loneliness is a dissonance
in a hollow cup.
Or a single black ant
losing the scent trail of its tribe.

It is a left-hand ring
with the collective broken heart
of all the world
in its vacant core.

This loneliness is a bamboo-cane spyglass
which is unable to focus.
Or a flit of wind
broken away from a storm.

It is a turtle
leaving a trail in dry sand across a continent
which has found nothing soothing
in which to dip its tongue.

This loneliness is a paint-chipped boat
once thumping against its mooring
abandoned on mudflats
waiting for an unreachable incoming tide.

It is a lone tiny Robin
singing its call
that receives
no response.

Not Writing Poetry

I threw moldy oranges
on my neighbor's roof
and worked hard to write a poem.
I just couldn't get inspired.

It occurred to me as I struggled:
writing poetry as popular as *Cheerios*
and as healthy as oats
may not really be good for you.

I decided to write with India Ink
but lo
the ink decided to return home.
I was left with a tabula rasa.

My next attempt failed
having left it on my car roof
running it over instantly killing
all of my profound thoughts.

A fine piece inked on onion skin paper
I went early to the coffee shop to edit
when a blind woman mistook its aroma
and crumpled it all over her salad.

My final attempt occurred
just as they ran out of toilet paper.
So there you have it for tonight
it was just not meant to be.

Line Dancing

Line dancing is shit and that's it!
Two words never meant to be paired.
The same goes for dance and square.
The universe is spiral. It's a gyre.

Galaxies, hurricanes, tornadoes,
dust devils, whirlpools, lightning,
the Chambered Nautilus, honeycomb,
sunflower seeds, Fibonacci.

Give me Whirling Dervishes,
The Twist, Gypsy Flamenco,
anything duende. Nothing linear.
Shall we dance? May I spin you?

Lichens

We are graciously hosted
by rock, trees and gravestones
who remind us that we
all live in relationship.

Ants each day pass by
and give us the latest news
which we pass to the Luna moth
for it has but a day to live.

We hide our friends
these ants and caterpillars
in our camouflage greens
from sight of Nuthatches.

We are slow and patient
and enjoy our mineral meals,
the shade and moisture
our exceptionally long lives.

Table Clock
> *I prefer the hell of chaos to the hell of order.*
>   — Wistawa Szymborska

At dinner time
it was all set
each nightfall
we figures
facing the table top.

Dad at twelve o'clock high
hands moving to flight lines
the plates so striking clean
before and after
and during the ritual meal.

Silence
infrequently broken
unspoken rules of Puritan pretense
passed around without question
reflected in our dishes.

Lifting a butter knife it is turned
so as to avoid reflecting sharply
the right eye
of the one who
is noon and midnight.

Sitting up straight
the cloth napkins in line
with the wristwatch
on his second hand
the artful limb constricted.

Compliance permits
no irregular attire
or condiments in unfit containers
that might jam the ticking precise
or reverent just-right talking.

Honoring Those in Uniform

Let's salute those in uniform.
Those deserving for their bravery,
risking their lives & health
so we feel safe, sanitized and secure.

Let's support our groups.
Those serving in our country,
those with hard hats and vests
bright green, orange and yellow.

Let's honor all those people
ALL those in uniform
who serve us each day
in their own honorable way:

Service station attendants
behind bullet-proof glass,
convenience store clerks;
pizza delivery drivers;

those wearing hazmat suits
preparing chemicals to keep
our toilets sparkling
our swimming pools aseptic;

cooks with burn marks
blade cuts and microwave damage;
bakers of our doughnuts
serving our coffee before sunrise;

utility pole climbers
and of wind turbines too;
those who unclog sewers;
those who install roofing;

movers of sleeper-sofas
and heavy book cartons;
those once called dog catchers
who lasso vicious street creatures;

cleaners of bathrooms
in unpleasant places:
rest areas, service stations
and fast-food joints;

Iron workers on skyscrapers;
highway construction folks;
those feathered First Peoples
who valiantly defend Turtle Island;

mechanics in repair shops
breathing exhaust fumes;
toll booth collectors;
miners; underwater welders;

delivery drivers unloading
heavy goods to our stores;
grocery clerks who hear
scanners in their sleep;

orderlies in hospitals
cleaning all kinds of disgust;
lab assistants; psych nurses;
flight attendants; bus drivers;

exotic dancers
whose uniforms are scant;
pharmacists; bar tenders;
poets with enchanted scarves.

Let's salute these who serve U.S.
with magnetic bowed ribbons
bumper stickers, license plates
and rallies at fairgrounds.

Let's honor these in uniform
with block parties and fireworks,
discount their airfare and meals
and televise their parade at *Disney World*.

PROSE POEMS

The Forest Where I Lived

The forest adjoined the back yard of my childhood home in Northeast Ohio. Although I spent a great amount of my childhood building balsa wood airplanes with my brother, younger sister and father in the basement, my real home was the fields, the woods and the forest. Similar memories would come to any other child who was from Munroe Falls in that time. Memories of the forest where I lived:

The ancient rotting tree. Forts dug in the ground or in the trees. Wild cherry tree sap near tree fort nails. Sassafras roots, twigs, bark, leaves, colors, beetles, grove. Crab Apple orchard. Moss. A garden. Leaves of all kind. Lots of leaves. The path cut through the deepest forest toward Riverview Elementary School.

The burn pile. Fire. And more fire. And the fire department trucks.

Aromatic Buffalo Grass. Enormous blackberry groves. Stinging Yellow Jackets. A Wolf Spider in its lair. A Luna Moth.

The bike trails. The mini-bike track.

A football field of 67 yards with a
furrow in the middle, tree stumps near
the sidelines and one tree-lashed goal
post. A line drive playing baseball
taking out both of my front teeth.

George whose garage abutted the field
who was an eccentric genius cash
register repair man. His wife who
yelled and stole our baseballs – and
our laughter as she drove her car
through the back of that garage
breaking hundreds of glass baby food
containers which held fasteners.

Headline: POETS FORCED TO EAT THEIR OWN WORDS

> *In a field....a newspaper has been lying for months
> ...aging because of days and nights, rain and sun.
> It's on its way to becoming...like an old memory
> changing into you.* – Tomas Tranströmer

All those clay figurines we someday poets formed
with minor hands. Between the thumb and index
finger we pinched them into shape. Most were not put
together well. Some toppled. All but a few were
globed back together in a muddy ball. Eventually they
were made into something else – or nothing at all.

Likewise made in the pressure point between those
two digits, is what we have written since. Again and
again it is for the most part nothing at all. A phrase
formed now and then, a concept worth saving at the
center of a bunch of gibberish. A little edible fruit
remains, hiding in what is of no meaningful value.

That remainder is like banana peels, egg shells, and un-kernelled cob ends. We have had piles of these scraps as writers, have we not: whatnot written on bar napkins and coasters, the backs of receipts and name badges, other people's business cards and the blank pages in their books? They are mottled together like succotash, the bits and pieces of lots of school lunch trays in one big heap on the corner of one's writing desk.

So into the designated post-writing shredder they go. Hashed and blended together, only a bit more indecipherable than when they went in. Then out to the compost bin, mostly the appearance of white hanging chads, garnished now with leaves and all of those previously mentioned organic residual leftovers. A small portion of mulch forms at the surface. Some settles to the bottom and forms clay.

In due season the loamy mixture is set about the garden for the next year. Or even for the season after that. Our writing all decomposes. The broken poems, broken ideas and broken lines are cultivated. And a transformation of energy ensues. New plants sprout. New flowers bloom. New bees arrive.

New fruit ripens, you eat it: the black raspberries, spinach, sweet corn, garlic, & carrots. We eat our own words.

Somehow, as you tilt your head gnawing on an ear of corn, you are inspired, struck by a notion. You write something new. Or this time you inscribe it into clay tablets. A new energy stirs within you. You start composing lyrics and poems again. A few are fruit. The remainder peels. And it starts all over.

If you find moldy rinds or un-kernelled cobs defining this sheet of pulp – just wait. This page is going somewhere else very soon.

The Hatfield

I first met Andy when he was near the old auction house in Clintonville, Kentucky. An unassuming character, Andy was a tall lanky guy who was a sun-dried 60ish. Each day he walked, brown bag lunch and thermos in the same strong hand, to the west for a few miles in the fields along Austerlitz Road, back and forth to work at the Lexington Bluegrass Army Depot.

What Andy did at the Depot I do not know. Perhaps he did very little. He could have done everything.

Andy was a Hatfield. Being from Kentucky as far back as he could remember, there may well have been a connection. His demeanor was kind and gentle as far as I could ever tell, seeking four-leaved clovers. And he sought them

On his daily stroll to and from work in the green months, Andy would scrutinize what grew in the fields along the country road he strode. And he did indeed find four leaf clovers. He found a lot of them. He would find four-, five- and even six- and seven-leaf clovers. He would pick the clover and place it in a brown paper sack about a fourth the size of his lunch bag. He would then remove his baseball cap, and carefully position the valuable memento between his brain and the underside of his bill.

And when he did get home he placed them under wax paper and ironed them to a cardboard.

Oh yes, Andy Hatfield found so many of those clovers that he wallpapered his entire house.

And maybe Andy was one of the luckiest men that I ever met, because he had an outlook that few I have met since ever do acquire. I'd say he was the real McCoy, but he was a Hatfield.

SELECTED LYRICS

from Music Projects

Grandfather's Mirror©

Nothing to Mend©

and

Online

All music available online at
www.reverbnation.com/boBHenning

Grandfather's Mirror
      in memory of Joseph DeVoe

I hold a photograph of you and me, with my sister and my brother.
There you are with your guitar – the father of my mother.
I ask, "Grandpa Joe, do you know how much you live in me now?"
Then I gaze into your mirror and I fix myself to go.

You lived upstairs your latter years all by yourself, alone.
And sometimes when I'd travel there to see you in your home,
you'd give to me a half a smile as I peered into your mirror,
and with your hand upon my head you'd say how much I'd grown.

When I was just a child you gave some gifts to me:
a love for playing six strings and telling a good story.
I wonder now if you ever knew the blessings you'd bestow,
when looking in this mirror you'd fix yourself to go.

It's many years since you've been gone and I have just begun,
to look inside where you reside, a place where we are One.
"Mirror, mirror on the wall tell me if you can,
will your glass provide some memories to quench this thirsty man?"

Ah, when I was just a child you gave some gifts to me:
a love for playing twelve strings and telling a good story.
I wonder now if you ever knew the blessings you'd bestow,
when looking in this mirror you'd fix yourself to go.

Legendary Bridge
      after Emma Jüng & Marie Louise von Franz's *The Grail Legend*

Chorus:
Bridge across the river only half way it extends.
Mounted in the middle unseen pillars to it tend.
Turning 'round on its own center a farther shore is spanned.
Passage to the other side – or back where I began?

Shackled in a dungeon or feasting in the king's great hall
biting kitchen cinders – ashes from the fire-fall
mesmerized by chamber maidens or guarding castle walls
all the while and everywhere a din of the spirit calls.

Chorus

Journeying 'cross a bridge of glass the cloud of fear descends.
Doubts of all my yesteryears attempt to apprehend me.
Continuing to travel soon I am aware that there's
another span before me – but half and arch from here to there.

Chorus

Upon a horse of four legs now halfway 'cross the watercourse
halting in the middle or at the end it seems
pausing for a moment my passage swings around.
Backing down the other side what was not built is found.

Chorus

It's hard to take a journey when you don't know whom you serve.
Am I just a soldier in a wounded king's reserve?
Or am I living dreams of knights beckoning me along
sent from minstrels of the king of kings of dusk and dawn?

Passage to the other side – or back where I began?

A Place to Call Your Own

There's a hidden room within this house
a place to call your own.
It was built with sighs and sacred eyes
and the loneliness that makes us wise.

You can go there any time you please –
the "Lost and Found" of all your needs.
A sanctum that contains no curse.
The still point of the universe.

There's enchantment in this hallowed room
a place where dreams abide.
Its entry but to you is known
a berth inside a welcome home.

There's a hidden room within this house
a place to call your own.
It was built with sighs and sacred eyes
and the loneliness that makes us wise.

Soul Mates

Would you walk a ways with me out under the moon?
If you can't I'll understand. Perhaps it's just too soon.
It's not that I have figured out what Autumn path to stride.
I'll still save you a place right by my side.

I live my life from day to day. I wonder how you are.
I think about your laughter and our search for shooting stars.
I wish I had some answers,
could heal your wounds and dry your eyes.
Perhaps one day we'll both grown bold and wise.

We've broken bread together. Taken journeys far and near.
Attempting to recover from lost affections haunting fears.
Through it all I've come to see you'll always be a part
of some substantial recess of my heart.

Shadow

Chorus:
There's someone following me.
So close that it gives me the creeps.
And it's not just at night in the pall of moonlight
but from dawn until dusk when the sun is so bright.
There's someone following me.

There's something so close behind me.
I could swear it's as if it's a part of me.
Like Captain Hook is to Peter Pan
or the woman who waits in the heart of a man
(the One who might offer a helping hand).
There's something so close behind me.

I want to follow the One who's gold as the sun
and whose light recasts my shadow.
To make amends – that silhouette befriend.
Meet at twilight's calm and dispel that old foe.

I've an inkling that there's more to be seen
when I turn 'round or look into my dreams
to catch a glimpse (though I sometimes wince)
has its own healing qualities.
I've an inkling that there's more to be seen.

If I find myself move from black, white to red
I then that figure will no longer dread,
a pathway will clear from my heart to my head
where silence is honored as much as what's said.

You (A Solace)
for Hillary Steckler

Another night
of too few dreams.
At dawn she lifts her head
from the pillow seams
raises her hands to fret her hair
then cups her face which is so fair
grabs a place in the world again.
It's not fair.

Kind'a like the way she is.
Fond of all the life she gives.
Pray she finds her own best way
into this
another day.

She's apparent as day for me.
Dispels the curse of dismay in me.
Lift your chin up and look right here.

Kind 'a like the way she is.
Fond of all the life she gives.
Pray she finds her own best way
into this
another day.

When the sun is low in the sky
and there's a solace glint in her eyes
you can sometimes see her dancing with me.
I will always save her the last dance
you see
you
I see it in you
I see it in you, the glint
I see it in you … I see it in you.

I'm Not Down with Clowns

Chorus:
At the carnival or at the circus.
From the parade downtown
to the county fair.
At the rodeo or at your neighborhood park.
Those clowns are everywhere.

Tall or small, kinky-haired or bald.
Their long-lobed ears and baggy pants.
Robust or lean and everything in between
at the sighting of clowns
I am appalled.

Holding rubber horns. Playing tiny tooters.
Driving small cars and little scooters.
Having fake fuzzy buttons
on the front of their frilly shirts.
Hands if they'd grab ya'
would really hurt.

Dark eyes so sad or just psycho and mad.
Ruffled collars holding rubber dollars.
Their noses rosy red
from brown bags they've sipped and fed.
And very, very
big shoes to fill.

Chorus

With their lollypops and whirligigs.
Knobby knees and oversize keys.
They tease. They squeeze.
They wheeze and make you ill at ease.

And all to the sound of a calliope.

At the carnival – with carnies
or at the circus – right behind you.
From the parade downtown – with Shiners
to the county fair – with cotton candy hair.
At the rodeo – by the barrels
or at your neighborhood park – behind the trees.
Those clowns are everywhere.
They're there. And there. And there.
Clowns scare me. Clowns scare me.
Keep those clowns away from me.
They may be funny to you – but not so for me.
Keep those clowns away from me!

Bugs on Drugs

Crickets whisper their story of plight
on a cool late summer night.
No one listens. No one cares ('bout)
the tale that crickets each nightfall share:
the bugs are on drugs. The bugs are on drugs.
All bugs are on drugs.

It explains why moths go to the light
and June Bugs flip in their flight
why Deer Flies always get in your hair
and Wolf Spiders (actually arachnids) have that stare.
The cicadas and locusts must be on crack.
The bugs are on drugs.
All bugs are on drugs.

Grasshoppers are spitting tobacco juice.
The Pill Bugs are all tryin' to get foot loose.
The bees have a buzz. The tics all have tics.
The mantis is praying for another fix.

They're smashed. They're trashed,
hashed and bashed.
The bugs are on drugs. They must be on drugs!

You're My Irish Blessing

Not many of us age like wine.
I was clearer sighted when I was ten.
Most people grow old like vinegar
and wish that they could be back when.

But once in a while there's an old soul
who with a young spirit lives on.

Chorus:
See the gleam in their eyes
and the way that they sigh.
There's a diamond refined in that mine.

Oh, life beats you down
and it's scary to see
someone younger than me
who's succumbed to the harsh realities
of how their life has played out to be.

But once in a while there's an old soul
who with a young spirit dreams on.

Chorus

It's sad and it's true and I miss you and …Ewe,
my memory is not all that good.
I forget and I fret and yet I regret that
I still like the best parts of you!

See the gleam in his eyes
and the way that he sighs.
There's a diamond refined in his mind.

So we gather alone in bars and in cars
and we worship in coffee shops too.
We share our sad songs but still sing along
'cuz what are we poor damn souls to do?

And once in a while there's that old soul
who with a young spirit sings on.

Chorus

Not many of us age like wine
as I said I was clearer when ten!
Most people grow old like vinegar
and wish that they could be back then.

But once in a while there's an old soul
who with a young spirit lives on.

Chorus

See the gleam in his eyes
and the way that he sighs.
There's a diamond refined …

Help Not Wanted (Pronoia)

'They' might think that you're paranoid
but people are out to help you.
The fact is you're just plain annoyed
with people always out to help you.

You try so hard but you can't avoid
people really out to help you.
They just can't stand that helpless void.
So people jump in to help you.

Look from the direction of everywhere
'cuz people are out to help you.
They come in bunches, dressed nice in pairs
with a mission they're out to help you.

You know the signs, you know the stare
when people are out to help you.
They want to. Need to. Have to care.
Those people are out to help you.

Please don't say, "May I help you?"
or call with a new loan rate fix.
Don't need no second helping
'cuz I'm already in a big fix
and I don't need another fix.

With a F.E.M.A. trailer and a bag of old ice
Somebody's out to help you.
Some new law or crack advice:
Big Brother's out to help you.

In suits, in robes, in white lab coats
they say that they're out to help you.
By The Book or with some votes
they promise that they're out to help you.

Please don't help me, please
I'm already in over my head.
Is my dis-ease really worse than some cures?
Mere words can't undo my dregs
False promises nothing but – said.

Gratitude

To corvids, anima, daemons, amusers, tricksters and psychopomps, and for exquisite support throughout this decade of work from The Indy Oatmeal Eaters: Marie Ursuy, Robin Walthery Allen and Jessica Kramer (*I am aware that it is not good to eat oatmeal alone – Galway Kinnell)*; Robert Bly who gave initial encouragement, sending personal thanks and good wishes especially for that "lively poem with good rat bones and doe skin in it;" publication and copy editor Tracy Catanese; prompts, writing and/or personal counsel, teaching insights and support of Matthew Dickman, Jean Shinoda Bolen, MD, PhD, Li-Young Lee, Jennifer Martin, Jay Leeming, Amanda Mosher, Peiyi Hu, MD, PhD, Martin Shaw PhD, Eleanor Wilner, Asher Elm-Hill, Hillary Steckler Barclay, Maggie Paul, Yiming Yang, OMD, MS, LAc, Mara-Lea Rosenbarger, Jamie Marie Rose, Cornelius Eady, Caroline Casey, Richard T. Miyamoto, MD, Jay Griffiths, Paul Kingsnorth, Nils Peterson, my resident alien wife Cindy and numerous creative souls of the Great Mother and New Father Conference.

To those already having gone ahead with Thanatos: Pierre Boivin, Tony Hoagland and Marion Woodman.

To the memories of my oldest sister, mother and father:

>Dixie Lee Worcester (1942–2009)
>Laura 'Lollie' Marie DeVoe (1923–2010)
>Robert Taylor Henning (1919–2013)

Finally, I look forward to the poems of Kate Dietz, Richard Lotni Elm-Hill, Chris Jansen and Marie Ursuy being published by an insightful benefactor. They have much rich earth to offer, and deserve to be heard and read. I will be honored to have each of them inscribe copies of these yet-to-be-unearthed rare metals for me before my ashes get planted under trees in Indianapolis.